GOATS
OF ANARCHY

LEANNE LAURICELLA
A.K.A. GOAT MAMA

ROCK
POINT

Quarto is the authority on a wide range of topics.

Quarto educates, entertains and enriches the lives of our readers—enthusiasts and lovers of hands-on living.

www.quartoknows.com

First published in the United States of America in 2017 by
Rock Point Gift & Stationery, a member of
Quarto Publishing Group USA Inc.
142 West 36th Street, 4th Floor
New York, New York 10018
www.quartoknows.com

10 9 8 7 6 5 4 3 2 1

ISBN: 978-1-63106-285-8

Editor: Chris Krovatin
Managing Editor: Erin Canning
Art Direction: Phil Buchanan
Cover and Interior Design: Sara Corbett
Photography: Leanne Lauricella

Printed in China

CONTENTS

Introduction 5

Cast of Characters 9

Babies 71

Goats Just Wanna Have Fun 89

Goat Yoga 107

The Snuggle is Real 125

The Enchanted Goat Forest 142

ME

LEANNE LAURICELLA

After several years of living and working in New York City, I began to crave more. Sure, the city was fun while I was young, single, and building a career, but I started to feel like my life was missing something.

After marrying my husband in 2011, I made the big move to New Jersey, and the country life was calling my name. I was a new vegan with a budding compassion for farm animals, and I wanted to learn more about them. While exploring my new town, I drove down many country roads and saw pastures of cows, sheep, and goats, and there was something about the goats that intrigued me. My husband and I visited a goat farm, and I felt an instant connection. I knew right then that I wanted goats of my own.

It was never my intention to rescue farm animals. I was still devoted to my career in the city as an event planner with no intention to retire any time soon. I had never heard of

farm animal sanctuaries, auctions, or online rescue sites as being accessible avenues for goat adoption, so I went to a local breeder for my first two goats. I read that most male goats are slaughtered very young, so I knew I should purchase two males.

I fell in love with my new babies, Jax and Opie, from the second I saw them. I was surprised at how easily we bonded, and the connection between us was exactly like it is between a human and a dog. Not only were they adorable and affectionate, but they were incredibly entertaining. I enjoyed watching their jumping, stomping, and playful head-butting, and the more time I spent outside with my goats, the more I resented my job. I found that doing farm chores outdoors was therapeutic. It wasn't long before I realized I was hooked, and two months later my two baby goats turned into five baby goats. I was having so much fun and wanted to share my daily goat adventures with the world, so I started an Instagram account called @goatsofanarchy. Within a few months, I had about three thousand followers who were enjoying the adorable photos and daily antics of my goats.

I found myself leading a double life: career girl by day and farm girl by night. The career girl in me was completely unfulfilled and thinking, "There has to be more to life than this." For years I spent every day, evening, and weekend working for someone else, helping them to succeed and fulfill their dreams, but what about my own? With my husband's blessing, I took a risk and quit my job. I knew I wanted to do something different, but as long as I was working, I had no time to figure out what that was. I was making a great salary, so quitting my job was scary for me. I was apprehensive about giving up some of the luxuries that I was accustomed to, but I knew I would adapt with time. On my very first day of unemployment, Instagram featured one of my photos on their home page and within hours, I acquired over thirty thousand new followers. I took this coincidence as a clear sign that I was on the right track!

April 1, 2014, was a day that set the path for the rest of my life as I agreed to take my first two rescue goats, Ansel and Petal. It was through the struggle to keep Ansel alive that I realized my empathy for special needs babies. My last twelve goats have either been sick, injured, or disabled, and I will continue to rescue baby goats who may otherwise be discarded because they have conditions requiring care that is very expensive or labor-intensive.

Goats of Anarchy, Inc., is now a 501(c)(3) non-profit organization. Our mission is to rescue and rehabilitate baby goats with special needs and provide them with a loving and happy forever home at our sanctuary. My message to you is to take a risk if you are feeling unhappy or unfulfilled in your life. Strive to do something selfless, and try to make the world a better place. Find what you love, and then do what you love.

JAX

CAST
OF
CHARACTERS

★ ★ ★ ★ ★ ★ ★

Get to know all the goats in the GOATS OF ANARCHY
family. The stories of how they came to me are sometimes
heartbreaking and I am endlessly inspired by how they
have persevered and found a special place in my heart.

JAX

★ ★ ★ ★ ★ ★ ★ **AND** ★ ★ ★ ★ ★ ★ ★

OPIE

A.K.A. THE OGS (ORIGINAL GOATS)

Jax & Opie are twin Nigerian Dwarf goats, born in April of 2014, and they were the first two members of the Goats of Anarchy gang. These two were such playful babies, and it was their energy, affection, and entertaining personalities that inspired my goat obsession. This is the photo that was featured by Instagram that made the Goats of Anarchy "goat famous."

JAX

Jax was the original alpha goat of the gang until Ansel the Destroyer came along. (You'll meet him later.) Jax loves his twin brother, Opie, and defends him in every goat battle. Jax is calm, intelligent, serious, and stubborn, but if I want to take a silly costume photo Jax is my guy.

OPIE

Opie is a lover with people, but he tends to get into scuffles with the other goats. He likes to remind the newcomers that he was here first! When Opie was about a year old, he fractured his elbow while playing. Today he walks with a slight limp, but he is very content lying out in the sun and relaxing with his friends.

NERO, TIG,
AND
OTTO

Only two months after welcoming Jax and Opie to our home, I knew I was hooked. What could possibly be better than two baby goats? Three baby goats! These three Nigerian Dwarf goats needed a home and I could not resist.

NERO

Nero and Tig are twin brothers. They were both disbudded, which means their horns were cauterized with a hot iron when they were only a few days old. Most of the time, when a male goat is disbudded, the horns start to grow back when the goat is about a year old. These are called scurs. Nero has a horn scur growing right in the middle of his head, so he is starting to look like a unicorn. He also has the longest, most fabulous beard of the herd, and he's pretty proud of it. Nero is a tough guy and loves a good goat battle, but it's all in fun.

TIG

A.K.A. THE CHEWER

Tig has always and will always be the first to put a hole through your shirt or chew off the ends of your shoelaces. He is relentless, but we forgive him because we love him so much. Tig almost died from pneumonia as a baby. Most people are under the assumption that goats are invincible, but they are actually quite susceptible to illness and disease. Tig has always kept himself out of trouble and gets along well with all of his goat friends.

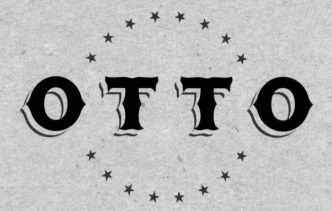

OTTO

After Jax and Opie, my husband agreed to let me get two more goats. I went to pick up twins Nero and Tig, but then there was little Otto. He looked like a tiny little black-and-white cow. How could I not take him? So, I had to tell my husband a little black-and-white lie, "Triplets!" I never told him about my scheme, but I guess he will find out soon enough! Otto was born polled, which means he was born without horns. Otto has always kept to himself, and although he is one of the heavier goats, he doesn't have a mean bone in his body and sometimes gets bullied. Otto loves attention from his human friends and loves to show his teeth when he smiles.

ANSEL

★ ★ ★ ★ ★ ★ ★ ★ ★ AND ★ ★ ★ ★ ★ ★ ★ ★ ★

PETAL

Ansel and Petal were rescued from a horrible cruelty case in New Jersey. The crime scene was called "the house of horrors" by the media. Two hundred baby farm animals were found starving and freezing, and piles of deceased animals were discovered throughout the property. Most of the surviving animals were infected with E. coli, including Ansel and Petal. They are not siblings, but they have been together since birth so they are best friends. Ansel and Petal were my first rescues, and it was the struggle to keep Ansel alive that made me realize my calling: to rescue sick, injured, or disabled baby goats.

ANSEL

A.K.A. THE DESTROYER

Ansel is a LaMancha goat. He is the largest goat in our herd right now, but he has the smallest ears, a defining characteristic of LaManchas. I adopted Ansel when he was only three days old, and he was critically ill with E. coli. His doctor was not sure he would survive, but after sleepless nights, IV fluids, vet visits, and medication, he pulled through! Watching this emaciated, sick, orphaned baby evolve into such strong, beautiful creature was life changing for me. I knew that I wanted to experience this over and over again. Ansel has earned the nickname "The Destroyer" because nothing is safe in his path. He will knock down, tear down, or chew anything he isn't supposed to. Such annoying characteristics have become quite endearing, and he is known and loved for them.

PETAL

A.K.A. QUEEN PETAL

Petal is a Saanen goat, a common dairy goat breed. Petal was also infected with E. coli, but her case was not as severe as Ansel's. Petal was Ansel's rock while he was sick, and she nurtured him the entire time. When I think of Petal, I think of girl power. She was the first female goat in our family, but she's just as tough as any of the boys. Petal has always been tough and daring. She is now referred to as the Queen because she often disciplines the boys and keeps things in order. She is beautiful and gentle, but she protects her kingdom.

JUICE

Juice was rescued from a local meat auction when he was only a few months old, and I fell in love with him the minute I saw him. He followed me around everywhere and practically begged me to take him home, and so I did. He is a pygmy goat with a raspy voice and horns that look like they were put on backwards. It took Juice a while to bond with the other goats, but now they are all great friends.

PROSPECT

A.K.A. THE GOAT WITH MANY COATS

Tiny little Prospect was born on a farm in New Jersey where he was rejected by his mother immediately after birth. Mothers often have an incredible sense when something is wrong, and she was right! Prospect was very sick and may not have survived without human intervention. Prospect was a day old and only weighed about a pound when I brought him home.

He was suffering internally with a severe impaction and in a great deal of pain. After a procedure at the vet, he was feeling like a healthy, happy baby goat. Prospect was born in in the winter and needed sweaters and coats to survive the brutal New Jersey weather and became known as The Goat with Many Coats. He had a coat for every occasion and then some. He is still very spoiled and vocalizes how much he hates sharing his food. Prospect is a little goat with a huge attitude.

POCKET

Pocket is a tiny little Nigerian Dwarf goat from Virginia who was born missing the bottom portion of both of his back legs. His prior owners were being encouraged to euthanize him until several Goats of Anarchy followers alerted me to the situation. His owners were excited to know that there was a bright future ahead for Pocket and happily surrendered him to us. Pocket is a happy, healthy baby goat and he is learning to walk on his little foam prosthetic legs. He is very young and will go through several pairs of prosthetics before he is fully grown. For now, Pocket lives in the house with his new best friend, Polly.

CHIBS

Chibs was born with contracted tendons in his front legs, causing his legs to curve inward. After a little time and exercise, the condition corrected itself and no treatment was needed. Chibs is one of the sweetest, most loving, happiest animals I have ever known. He has always been very gentle with his sister, Lyla, and is very protective of her. If they are separated for even a minute, they call to each other. The twin bond is very strong.

★ ★ ★

LYLA

A.K.A. PRINCESS LYLA

Lyla was born missing her entire left leg, hip bone, and part of her pelvis. She also had a little hole in her belly that was leaking urine, which we had surgically corrected. Lyla had a tough time finding her balance as a baby, but when she finally got the hang of it she was unstoppable. Lyla is a very sweet, happy little girl, and she doesn't let her disability slow her down. She climbs, jumps, and plays with the rest of them, and she is the first one to challenge a new goat when they join the herd. Lyla loves her brother Chibs more than anything, and she rarely leaves his side.

ANGEL

Angel is a fainting goat who was born on a small farm in Kentucky on
February 13, 2016. Her mother escaped the farm to give birth, and the
owners found them the next day. Angel was frozen to the ground and thought to
be deceased until she let out a faint little cry. She was rushed to a warm bath, but
unfortunately the damage was already done. She lost the tips of both ears and both
back legs due to frostbite. Her little body suffered incredible trauma, but she is a
fighter and has overcome so many obstacles in her short life. Angel has been slow to
develop in every way, but she is now thriving. She loves her cart and loves her other
special needs goat friends. Angel is a true inspiration to all of us.

MARILYN

Marilyn is a Boer goat from Michigan who was listed for sale on Craigslist because of an injury she sustained as a baby. The injury caused Marilyn to eventually lose her foot, and her weight gain made it increasingly difficult to walk. Marilyn was a family pet, destined for slaughter because of her disability. Marilyn is very friendly and enjoys affection. She just received her pretty pink prosthetic foot and she loves it!

ALLEY

Alley is a tiny little lady who weighs only about forty pounds. She was repeatedly impregnated, and her babies were sold at a local meat auction. While trying to escape from the prison she was living in, Alley caught her eyelid on a chain-link fence. A piece of the wire from the fence pierced through her eyelid, and she was unable to free herself. A Goats of Anarchy Instagram follower happened to pass by and heard Alley's screams. Thankfully, the follower was able to free Alley with wire cutters, and then alerted me to the situation. Alley's eye was untreated for several days until we could finally rescue her, but she has healed perfectly. Alley runs around as fast as she can, expressing pure joy and freedom. She is still fearful of humans but making great progress. She knows that she is safe now.

ABEL

Abel was only about a month old at the time of his rescue. Both of his back hooves were injured, and he could barely walk. Our vet concluded Abel's legs must have been tangled in wire or string for some time, and we feared he would lose one of them. Fortunately, Abel made a full recovery, and today he is running and jumping all over the farm. Abel is very playful with the other goats but never leaves his mother's side.

MILES

A.K.A. MAMA'S BOY

Miles is a Kiko-Boer cross who suffered from a condition that is sadly too common among baby goats. He had extremely contracted tendons in his front legs. In less severe cases, like Chibs', the tendons will straighten on their own, or with physical therapy. Both of Miles' front legs were completely curled underneath him, causing him to walk on his face. Thankfully I have a wonderful, courageous veterinarian who was willing to take on the challenge. After an experimental surgical procedure, we were thrilled with the outcome. Miles now walks upright with two straight legs! He endured a painful surgery with months of rehabilitation, and yet he is one of the happiest goats in the gang. No one loves a hug more than Miles and I am sure that even when he weighs two hundred pounds, he will still find a way to sit in my lap.

LINC

Linc is a LaMancha goat who was born on the same farm in southern New Jersey where Prospect was born. When Linc was about six weeks old, one of the workers on the farm ran over his leg with a pickup truck. Rather than seek medical attention, they splinted his leg with a cardboard toilet paper roll. Medical care was not a priority because he was destined for slaughter. Linc came to live with us almost two weeks after his injury, and our vet confirmed that his leg was broken. Linc is still skeptical of humans, but he is realizing that not all of us are bad, and he will come around when he is ready.

PILOT

Pilot's story is very similar to Angel's. He is a fainting goat who was born on a small farm in Minnesota, only two days before Angel was born. His mother also escaped her enclosure to give birth, and the result was frostbite for baby Pilot. He lost both of his ears and the bottom portions of both back legs. Pilot struggled to keep up with his mother on the farm and often fell behind. He learned to walk on his two front legs, but he had trouble when he started gaining weight. His owners surrendered him to Goats of Anarchy when he was around five months old. Pilot was transported from Minnesota to New Jersey by the Pilots N Paws® program. He traveled on four small private planes to get to us. Pilot loves his new legs and runs like he's been waiting to run for his entire life. This once timid and shy little goat is now bursting with confidence.

POLLY

A.K.A. POLLY POCKET

Polly has already stolen thousands of hearts across the world. She is a Nigerian Dwarf goat who was born blind. She came to us at seven weeks old when her previous family realized her special needs were more than they could provide. Polly was born with a neurological disorder that may have been the cause of her blindness. Fortunately, she does have light and shadow sensitivity so this keeps her from running into things. Polly lives in the house and loves nothing more than snuggling on the couch with a big blanket.

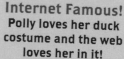

Internet Famous!
Polly loves her duck costume and the web loves her in it!

★ ★ ★

AUGGIE

✦ ✦ ✦ ✦ ✦ ✦ ✦ ✦ AND ✦ ✦ ✦ ✦ ✦ ✦ ✦ ✦

JUNE

Auggie and June are twin Nigerian Dwarf goats who were born on a small farm in Wisconsin. Auggie's front legs are extremely bowed with both shoulders displaced, causing his front legs to go straight out to the side like a bird. The bones in his legs are curved, so splinting will not work. Auggie's condition is severe, but he has had a surgery commonly performed on foals to stimulate bone growth. He wears a harness to help retrain his shoulders, and over time, we expect to see great results! June is perfectly healthy, but I can never separate twins, so we took her too! June is small but mighty and has absolutely no fear! She always looks out for her brother Auggie and they are inseparable.

CHERRY

Cherry is a baby Boer goat from a farm in New Jersey. Since birth, Cherry has always been a little "off." Her prior owner said she was unable to nurse from her mother and had a very hard time with the bottle as well. They thought she might even be blind because she would often get lost. Cherry has been diagnosed with a severe neurological disorder which may have caused her limited vision and social debilities, but she loves being cuddled in her afternoon naps, and is perfectly happy living in what we call "Cherry's world."

RUBY

Ruby is a Nigerian Dwarf goat who was found as a newborn, all alone, near the Ruby Mountains in Nevada. There was no sign of her mother, or anyone else nearby, so rescuers took her home and worked to save her. Unfortunately, she lost both ears and the ends of both back legs to frostbite. Ruby's owners realized that they were unable to provide her with the long-term care that she needed and agreed to send her to us. With the help of wonderful volunteers, Ruby made the long cross-country drive to New Jersey and is currently awaiting her first set of prosthetic legs!

GRACE

Grace was the victim of a cruel abuse situation in Arkansas. A group of high school senior boys rented her for $10 from a friend to use her as entertainment for their party. They smashed beer cans over her head, dragged her around with a rope, taunted her, and fed her cigarette butts. She became so ill in the days following that it was rumored she had died. We sent a volunteer to Arkansas to pick her up and drive her back to New Jersey. She was severely dehydrated, covered in lice, and emaciated. She had scratches in both eyes and a horrible upper respiratory infection. Grace was in terrible condition, but she has made a full recovery and is enjoying her new life with us. For the rest of her life, Grace will know nothing but love and security, and will go to bed with a full tummy every night.

PINEY

★ ★ ★ ★ ★ ★ ★ AND ★ ★ ★ ★ ★ ★ ★

WINSTON

Piney, AKA the Goat Nanny, was surrendered by his former owner when he was about three months old. Until recently, he lived in the house with us, but he realized his calling when we rescued Lyla and Chibs. He adored Lyla, and seemed to understand the fragility that came with her physical struggles, so he was very gentle with her. His new buddy, Winston, was found trapped in a cage with a dog and a baby goat in the alley of a used-car lot in Newark, New Jersey. Thankfully, we were alerted, and were able to rescue them. For a while after we got him, he was convinced Piney was his mama! Now the two pigs live together as best friends in their pig palace outside the barn.

ROMEO
★ ★ ★ ★ ★ ★ ★ · AND · ★ ★ ★ ★ ★ ★ ★
TORRES

Romeo (the mini horse) and Torres (the mini donkey) have lived together their entire lives and came to Goats of Anarchy when they were both around eleven years old. They are inseparable and must be within sight of each other at all times. They love all of the goats, but they were recently given their own space because they also love to eat the goats' food! Both are gentle and affectionate. Romeo is recognized for his frizzy, wild hair and Torres is known for his curvaceous figure.

BABIES

Baby goats are just about the cutest thing
on the planet. These often wild little ones
are charming, cute, and oh so naughty.

MILES had just arrived home from the hospital after having his surgery and was getting used to those big, heavy splints on his front legs. It was so exciting to walk upright for the first time but also a lot of work. Nap time!

POLLY is blind, but she still needs her exercise. There is absolutely nothing weird about walking a blind baby goat in a diaper and onesie on a leash!

CHIBS and his twin sister, LYLA, came to us in the middle of winter, so they lived in the house for a couple of months. They wore diapers, for obvious reasons, and baby onesies to keep the diapers on. CHIBS was out on the deck experiencing snow for the first time, and that smile on his face shows just how he felt about it.

POCKET received a pocket sized goat of his own and could barely contain his excitement!

Because LYLA was so special, and just a little spoiled, we used to snuggle together on the window seat to watch the snow fall.

ANGEL may not have back legs, but she has a fabulous pink cart. Just look at that confidence!

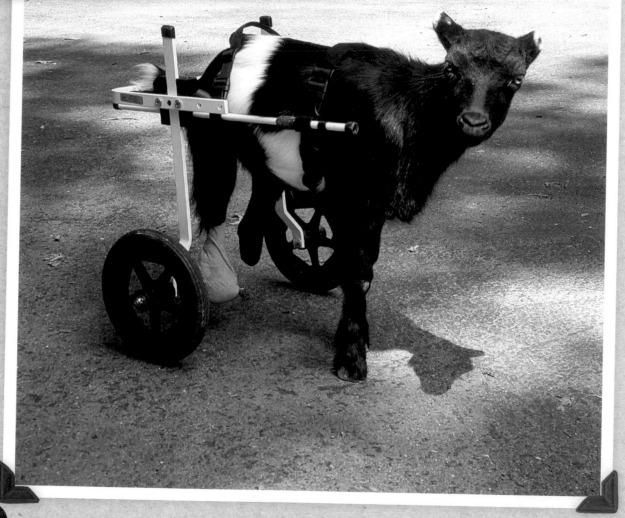

PILOT wasn't able to run for the first five months of his life. When he got his new cart, he took off like he had been waiting for that moment forever.

Only hours after **PETAL**'s rescue from a horrific cruelty and neglect case, she was bright-eyed and ready to take on the world. This was her expression the first moment we met.

Twins **CHIBS** and **LYLA** are always together. They eat together, play together, sleep together, and even pose together.

Because POLLY is blind, her pupils are always dilated, which causes her to look like a stuffed animal. Who needs a garden gnome when you have POLLY the beautiful garden goat?

This expression should have warned me about sweet little PROSPECT. He has so much attitude packed into that tiny little body of his.

Having only three legs has never stopped **LYLA** from being a brave, silly, and spunky little girl. She doesn't let anything hold her back.

PROSPECT was a very spoiled only child living in the house with my husband and me until **CHIBS** and **LYLA** arrived. It took a little bit of time, but eventually he learned to share, and now the three of them are inseparable.

BABY NERO is so cute standing on the patio chair that you barely even notice the puddle he left underneath!

Pretty **POLLY** doesn't need to see. She's the only thing worth looking at anyway.

OTTO is an old soul who knows how to enjoy life to the fullest. Why stop to smell the flowers when you can eat them?

GOATS
JUST WANNA
HAVE FUN

★ ★ ★ ★

You never have to worry about goats taking themselves too seriously. Talk about a wacky, fun-loving group, full of personality. From Popsicles to beach chairs, there is nothing stopping these goats from having a great time. Boredom is not an option.

People often ask if goats like to have fun in the snow. Well, **JAX** and **OPIE** definitely like to eat it!

Sometimes we need to break up a boring day with something special, and there is nothing more special than a streamer party with **JAX, OPIE, NERO, OTTO,** and **TIG** (my first five goats)!

ANSEL THE DESTROYER will literally destroy anything in his way, even an innocent little snowman. To **ANSEL**, this is pure entertainment.

Some of the goats are goofier than the others. **PETAL** always finds a way to make me laugh. Feeling blue? Spend some time with **PETAL** and she'll show you life through her blue-tinted glasses.

A goat and his ball. This is the beginning of something special.

On a hot summer day, the goats love a cold snack as much as we do. **CHIBS** is always the first goat to come running for Popsicle time!

PRINCESS LYLA is a natural beauty, but she knows how to spice it up with the perfect accessories!

ANGEL has conquered many obstacles in her life. This giant ball doesn't faze her at all.

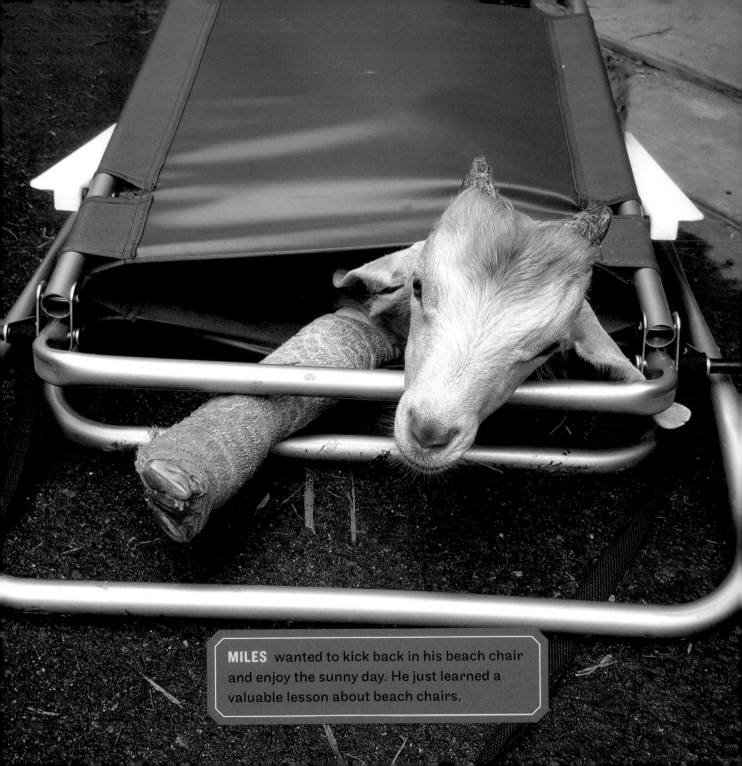

MILES wanted to kick back in his beach chair and enjoy the sunny day. He just learned a valuable lesson about beach chairs.

JAX and OPIE are twins, but on their birthday, JAX likes to pretend he's an only child.

PETAL's favorite goat game is hide and seek. She likes to close her eyes and count while everyone else hides.

CHIBS doesn't fully understand the concept of milking. He saw photos and thought he would try it out himself.

ANSEL isn't playing dress–up; this is just how he looks before a long goatorcycle ride.

The long jump is **OTTO**'s favorite category in the goat Olympics.

PROSPECT is putting the finishing touches on the decorations for his favorite annual event, Goatchella.

Oh, **CHIBS**! I guess there really is no way to have a goat-proof flower garden!

GOAT YOGA

★ ★ ★ ★

My goats are hip to all the latest trends, including incorporating the calming effects of a little morning yoga (well, sort of). Take a look to at these goats as they work their sun salutations into their barnyard routines.

POLLY is feeling very Zen right now.

OPIE hasn't quite mastered the chaturanga flow just yet.

ANGEL is such a determined little baby. She tried to do yoga all by herself.

Apparently, **JAX** misunderstood what it means to work on your core.

MILES can't wait to start doing yoga once his legs have healed. He's already picked out his yoga shirt!

ANSEL teaches sunset vinyasa to the rest of the gang.

113

It's so embarrassing when you get an itch during yoga class.

"You guys go ahead without me; namastay right here and take a nap."

OTTO has mastered the
happy baby goat pose!

This pose is called the bend and snack.

JUICE is getting a little back scratch during his sun salutations.

Sometimes meditation makes **MILES** sleepy.

This must be freestyle yoga with **JAX** . . . because otherwise , I have no idea what he's doing!

CHIBS needs a little more practice finding his center.

PETAL got the munchies during her downward facing goat pose.

THE
SNUGGLE
IS
REAL

★ ★ ★ ★

Goats may seem rough around the edges, but don't let the horns fool you—these sweethearts love a good snuggle. Whether it's cuddling with another goat, a human, or even a pig, the GOATS OF ANARCHY never turn down a chance to get down and comfy with friends and family.

About a week after their rescue, **CHIBS** and **LYLA** snuggled together with big smiles on their faces. They knew they were home.

PINEY THE GOAT NANNY shouldn't have favorites, but he really loves ANGEL. The two of them snuggled by the fire every day for months.

The first time **ANGEL** and **POLLY** spent time together, this happened.

While rehabilitating together, **MILES** and **ANGEL** fell in love.

From day one, **CHIBS** has always had **LYLA**'s back.

Even **ROMEO** had to get in on the snuggles. Everybody loves **ANGEL**.

CHIBS and **LYLA** demonstrate something called a cuddle puddle.

MILES' love for ANGEL is undeniable.

ANGEL and PILOT are the same breed, the same age, have the same injuries, and the same smiles. Fate has never been so adorable.

This is the only way a pig and a goat should roast by a fire.

A true friend is someone you can lean on, literally.

Now that's a party bucket! **POLLY** and **ANGEL** don't care where they cuddle, so long as they can take it easy.

They even cuddle while they drink!

"That's enough, MILES!"

ELLA

During the publication of this book, I lost one of my babies. Ella's passing taught me a valuable lesson: that no matter how hard I try, I cannot save them all. Ella came to us emaciated, anemic, and unable to eat on her own, but that did not stop her from fighting. I will never forget her adorable fuzzy face and sweet spirit. Ella's passing was a shock and I will never forget her.

Ella passed away in my arms on November 30, 2016.

Ella, your life mattered and you will not be forgotten.

THE ENCHANTED GOAT FOREST

★ ★ ★

All of the goats live peacefully together at Goats of Anarchy. The larger, healthier goats are very accepting of the goats with physical disabilities.

Our wonderful group of volunteers built our goat playground. They have a full-size sunken trampoline with a deck surrounding it. Every morning and every evening the goats run to the trampoline deck to play head-butting games. There are steps, ramps, bridges, and forts throughout the playground.

★ The Enchanted Goat Forest is full of yummy trees for the goats to snack on. Goats are foragers and do not typically eat grass. They prefer brush, weeds, and trees.

★ The goats even have their very own goatorcycle!

★ Because goats are herd animals, they usually do everything together. They eat together, nap together, sleep together, and most importantly... they play together!

ACKNOWLEDGMENTS

Many thanks to everyone at Quarto Publishing, especially my editors Rage Kindelsperger and Chris Krovatin for their patience and guidance during the writing of my first book.

A million hugs and thank-yous to all of my social media followers. Goats of Anarchy, this book, and the work I love doing would not exist without your support and appreciation. I literally could not have done it without you.

Heaps of gratitude to all my fellow rescuers for their advice and counsel, and to all of my friends who offer up their time and talent to help around the farm. Without your help I wouldn't have been able to succeed at it (or find the time to write this book!).

Thanks so much to my family, especially my parents, for all their love and encouragement. And finally, thank you to my husband, Billy, for being so supportive of this crazy dream of mine and putting up with the revolving door of baby goats we've had living in our house. I love you.

EPILOGUE

Many people ask me for advice on getting started with rescue. The best advice I can give is to start small. Start with two animals and make sure you are ready for the commitment. I have given my life to saving those who cannot speak up for themselves and it is a full-time job. Rescue is very rewarding and, yes, there are tons of hugs and snuggles involved, but choosing a life of rescue is choosing a life that is no longer your own.

There will be no more sleeping in on the weekends, and you can kiss those vacations good-bye. You will battle feelings of hopelessness, depression, exhaustion, and sadness, but the rewards far outweigh all of that. There is no better feeling than to watch those animals grow, heal, and learn to trust again.

Not everyone is called to rescue, but that doesn't mean you can't help. Rescues need donations and volunteers. I want to encourage everyone to research factory farming and then find some way to spend time with farm animals. You can also help by living as cruelty-free as possible. Again, start slow—try giving up meat, and then one day dairy products, leather, and products tested on animals. Please help me save the world, one goat at a time!

Photo by Jana Kirn.